Dr. Anindita Dutta is a University teacher and a writer in the area of English Language Studies & Corporate Communication. Her areas of interest and specialisation include, Corporate & Digital Communication, English Language Studies, 21st Century Skills and Current Trends in ELT. In her book, 'Mastering the Presentation Moment', Dr Dutta brings her 23 years of experience on how to present as a professional with ease and elan. In her book, she presents compelling insights and practical examples on how to take one's career to the next level through effective strategies of presentation.

Copyright © Dr. Anindita Dutta, 2023

Mastering the Presentation Moment
by Dr. Anindita Dutta
Paperback Edition

First Published in 2023 by

Inkfeathers Publishing
Vivek Vihar, New Delhi 110095
www.inkfeathers.com

ISBN 978-81-19483-35-8

All rights reserved. No part of this book may be reproduced, lent, resold, or transmitted in any form or by any means, electronic or mechanical, including photocopying, recording, or by any other information storage and retrieval system, without permission in writing from the publisher.

MASTERING THE PRESENTATION MOMENT

For Students & Professionals

DR. ANINDITA DUTTA

Inkfeathers Publishing

www.inkfeathers.com

To my dear students...

ACKNOWLEDGEMENTS

I extend my thanks to the entire publishing team for their support and guidance in publishing this book.

I take this opportunity to say a big thank you to my family and friends for their love and unconditional support…To my late father, who has been my mentor and my greatest source of strength…I miss you beyond measure. To my lovely mother, who has been there for me through the highs and lows of my life. To my husband, for being my best friend and inspiration and for letting me be. To my sons, for their love, appreciation and encouragement. I feel very blessed to have you all.

I would like to remember with love and reverence my teachers and professors, my educators, who have taught me with sincerest dedication the lessons from books and life and the importance of human values that helped me be what I am today. I owe it all to you.

Finally, I would love to thank the amazing people I work with, my co-workers, colleagues, and my dear students. Working with you all, has enriched me in every way.

CONTENTS

INTRODUCTION

Great communicators have extraordinary capabilities of influencing people in life and work. In this age of digital revolution and global connectivity, we need to learn how to present the most important and intricate piece of information in a simple but effective manner. This could pose a challenge to many. However, careers now reach new heights with effective skills of communication, particularly in business and profession. The skill of presenting has become an essential tool in academic and professional communication. The credibility of any presented talk is doubled with the addition of relevant visual images that help communicate a message better. A presenter may be a confident speaker and entertaining to hear. But despite his knowledge of a chosen subject, his talk may not reach out to the audience due to a lack of persuasiveness, clarity, and poor visuals. On the contrary, a presenter who can deliver a well-structured talk supported by appropriate visuals is easy to understand. This blending of the verbal and the visual can therefore create a visual story that validates a talk that is being presented.

A presentation can somewhat be compared to a movie. The only difference is that a presentation supported by slide visuals is up, close, and personal in comparison to a movie. The audience in a presentation remains close to the scene of action, and the actors (presenters here) get the opportunity of interacting 'live' with the audience. Presentation through Power Point, therefore, stands out not merely as a visual treat to the audience but as a complete package as the presenter's speech combines with visual images. With relevant images, speech becomes stronger and more impactful. A picture we know is worth a thousand words, a maxim that holds great significance when it comes to making presentations through visual support.

Presentations are now indispensable in academic and workplace communications. The acquisition of the skills of presentation may begin in a classroom but goes much beyond it. A presentation not only helps a student to gain real-world skills but teaches how to communicate complex information in simple, interesting, and understandable ways. Through presentations, students and professionals gain opportunities to develop skills in real-world communications. This improves their speaking abilities in ways that can be advantageous for their academic growth and future employment. Presentation skill is now considered to be one of the major 21st-century skill that hiring managers look for in a candidate, something that could bring about a significant career progression.

PRESENTATION: WHAT AND WHY

A presentation is a brief interesting talk on a topic delivered to a group of people in an academic or professional setting. It is a kind of speaking engagement that can be modified to a variety of speaking situations, such as talking to a group, making a speech, teaching, and learning in class, briefing a team, or getting a point across to an audience in a seminar or conference. It is typically a lecture or speech with relevant visual supports meant to inform or raise awareness on some important issues, to demonstrate a product, to teach or learn in a classroom setting, to present a seminar or conference paper, to explain and share data, even to sell and market.

However, the greatest presenter of all time, Steve Jobs, has transformed the very meaning of the word 'presentation'. What looked like some kind of a dull and monotonous slide show turned into a theatrical event with stunning stage crafts. Listening to Jobs' presentation was an extraordinary experience for his audience; he would create a kind of theatrical performance for them.

Presenting is an important employability skill that most people need in their world of work. The skill of presentation prepares a student for the workplace. Whatever profession students plan to take up in future, the skills of presentation will play a pivotal role in that. Students, therefore, need ample opportunities to practice language in situations that encourage them to communicate and present their needs, ideas, and opinions. In the future, most learners are going to take up varied professions. Some may take up marketing jobs, it is therefore important for them to learn the skills of presenting that are exclusive to product promotion, demonstration, and marketing. Others, who may opt for teaching and research, will utilise presentation skills as a part of classroom teaching, learning, and research. Again, those who intend to join the industry need to learn the art of making boardroom presentations and client presentations that would form an integral part of corporate culture.

The job scenario today demands that every candidate who aspires for a coveted job must be well- equipped with the skills of communication and presentation. The existing workforce and the future generation need to develop themselves as effective communicators, critical thinkers, innovators and problem solvers. They need to adapt skills and capabilities to fulfil the demands of the global market. Presentation is a useful priority skill for students attending a college or university. Academic and research papers require learners to give a variety of presentations. Students attending college or university, therefore, gradually get to learn how to transfer knowledge through the skills of presentation from classrooms to the workplace, from an academic set-up to a professional one.

Learning how to design effective presentations helps one develop insightful thinking. In the process, learners transform themselves into confident presenters learning how to inform, explain and persuade in the most effective manner. With rapid globalization, fresh young graduates just out of college need to be proficient in effective communication and presentation skills for placements, career promotion, and growth. It is this skill of presentation that helps to bridge the gap between language study and language use.

The chapters in the book manifest unique approaches of creating and delivering powerful presentations in a simple and concise manner. They highlight effective ways of delivering visual stories and presenting them as a true professional. There are valuable insights on how to keep the audience spellbound throughout a presentation.

1

THE BEGINNING: PLANNING & RESEARCH

A successful presentation begins with proper planning and research. As a presenter, you must first choose a topic and write down the objectives of your presentation in a single concise statement. In other words, it is important to write down the desired outcome of your presentation. This will help you as a presenter to narrow your focus and reach your goal.

Planning A Presentation

Depending on the aims, the structure and shape of a presentation vary significantly. Here are some key stages to plan a presentation:

- Selecting a topic
- Researching
- Aims & Objectives
- Knowing the audience

- Defining the key message statement
- Crafting a message
- Outlining the scope
- Preparing the presentation script
- Using visual support
- Presentation Delivery

How to Research a Topic

At the very beginning, it is important to research and collect facts on a chosen topic. It is necessary to create an outline of your presentation on the basis of your research. There can be a wide variety of sources that you can explore in order to research on the subject selected.

1.   Library

This could be your primary source of research and could provide necessary data if carefully browsed. You could access your institute or office library, which probably has a wide range of reference materials.

2.   Peer-Reviewed Academic Journals

Irrespective of the topic of your presentation, consult multiple journals to support your research efforts.

3.   Google Scholar

Google Scholar provides a search for a wide range of

journals and other academic articles.

4.   Google Patent Search

Google Patent Search permits you to look through licenses, and this can now and again give the ideal visual to your show.

5.   Newspapers

Google News search allows you to search newspaper archives, some of which could even be traced back 150 years or more.

6.   Dictionaries And Other Reference Books

A wide range of dictionaries and reference books could be valuable sources. Be sure you are going through some authentic publications before citing material.

7.   People

Sometimes the most valuable speech topic research could be found among the people in your life. Try to find such people, interview them carefully, and quote them accurately.

8.   Wikipedia

The world's largest and most comprehensive encyclopedia could be a good source initially to gain some familiarity with a topic that you have selected to present. However, encyclopedias are tertiary sources and are generally considered a weak resource.

9. Authentic Online Resources

All online resources may not be authentic and trustworthy. It is always better to opt for official sites whenever you can. It is always advisable to refer to government websites, for, say, some comprehensive demographic statistics, instead of any random website whose affiliations may be fake.

The prerequisites for any presentation are, therefore, research and knowledge of the subject to be presented. Preparation carries with it a kind of passion that is a powerful component to effectively present. Presentation is all about entertaining and conveying information to the audience. Whatever the subject, a presenter must try to find ways to make the content and delivery enjoyable. Even the driest of subjects can be lifted to an extraordinary level through research, imagination, clarity, and visuals.

During the planning stage, it is best to put aside detailed research notes. Instead, prepare a list or summary of the main points expressing each point in a few words or a short sentence. As a presenter, try to find answers to the following questions: "What should be the takeaway from this presentation?" The answers to these questions will help any presenter communicate clear and effective messages to the audience. After having identified the main points, it is now important to embellish them with supporting information.

Identifying your presentation's precise objective is the first step in the planning process. From the very onset, be clear on the aim of your presentation so as to stay focused. This not only builds up your confidence but helps you remain in control of the presentation you are about to deliver. At this preparatory stage, try to single out your audience (students, professors, academicians, experts, industry people, and the like) before whom you are about to present.

The next important step is to determine how well you can organise, structure, and deliver a presentation within a given time frame. It must not be forgotten that a presentation is bound by time, and you are set to create the maximum impression in a minimum amount of time.

2

STRUCTURING A PRESENTATION

What makes a presentation well-structured? A structure is the backbone of any presentation and must be created keeping in mind the crux of a topic and the message it conveys. Many people come up with great ideas but are unable to express themselves as they do not have a definite structural plan. The message could be simple or complex, short, or long, but it must be presented essentially in an articulate and understandable manner. It is important for learners to understand that messages of any type can be delivered through a simple and clear presentation. While presenting, build up an easy-to-understand core message that the audience will be able to remember even after the presentation gets over. It is recommended, therefore, that a presenter prepares a draft, sketching rough ideas for a presentation first on paper. The best presenters spend a considerable amount of time thinking, sketching, and scripting. As a presenter, set aside only one-third of the time in designing your slides. Dedicate the rest of your time to researching the topic, collecting inputs from experts, organizing ideas, collaborating with team-mates, and sketching the structure of the story.

The Organising Part

To organise a presentation, it is necessary to sequence the arguments logically. A presentation could be structured into four parts: an opening, a descriptive body that can possibly address the problem at hand, the proposed solution with a call to action, and finally, a proper conclusion. In one of his famous presentations, for example, Steve Jobs structured his presentation speech by using the rule of three. He divided his speech into three simple parts:

a) The first part—the opening

b) The second part—he shared three of his personal stories and

c) The third part—he ended his presented talk with a suitable conclusion.

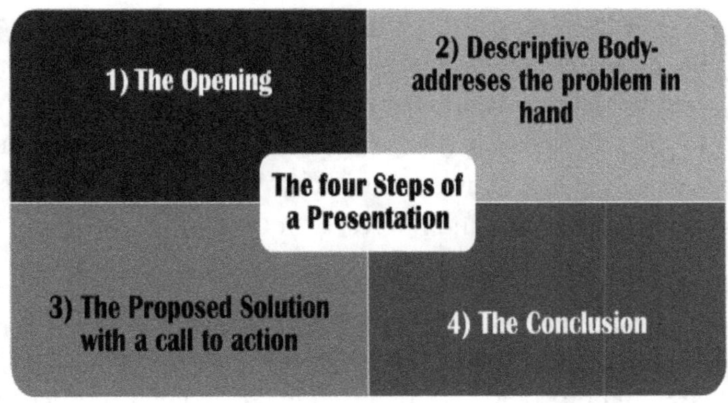

Since the presentation is a formal talk, explain ideas or information in a clear, structured way. A presentation is structured with the following:

a) *An interesting and informative introduction.*

b) *A series of points presented sequentially in a logical manner in the body.*

c) *A proposed solution.*

d) *A lucid and purposeful conclusion and a summarizing of the key areas covered.*

Preparing the Body of the Presentation

Structure the body of a presentation first. It is important to bring variety to the body of a presentation so that listeners do not face boredom with too many facts, statistics, or data. While structuring the body of a presentation, make an outline of your talk, state the key ideas, and elaborate them with sufficient illustrations. Visual aids are added to engage and keep alive the interest of the audience.

The body forms the longest part of your presentation; elaborate the chief points to the audience in the best possible manner. Here is where the ideas are presented with clarity. To present ideas with conviction, illustrate and support them. The supporting information and the relevant case studies add colour and interest to your talk.

Sequencing a presentation gives it a smooth flow. The information presented in the body must be well-structured through an organizing principle. Alternately, the body of a presentation could be sequenced in chronological order on the basis of theme or in order of importance. The type of presentation a presenter would make—informational, persuasive, or explanatory—will determine which organization pattern he should follow.

The **chronological order** works best for *explaining* a process and simultaneously taking an audience through the steps gradually. This structure also gives the presenter an opportunity to interact with the audience, fielding their questions or comments after each step.

The **comparison/contrast pattern** is best suited for two different (or similar) subjects. This pattern is effective for an *informational* presentation but can also help to *persuade* an audience to make a choice.

Past problem to future solution: In this pattern, the presenter could describe how things once were and how they need to be in the future. This sequence could be used to recommend a new direction or course of action and to highlight how the future will be different from and better than what it once was.

General to Specific: This kind of presentation moves from general information to in-depth explanations of a few key points. Sometimes it begins with a main idea and then elaborates on how to make the main idea work. An order of importance would allow a presenter to present ideas, moving either from the least to the most important point or vice versa. This may be used for either *informational* or *persuasive* presentations.

Once you have prepared the body of your presentation, decide how to begin and end a presentation talk. Your introduction needs to capture the attention of the audience, and your conclusion summarise and reiterate the important points.

3

HOW TO START & END A PRESENTATION

The delivery of a good presentation depends on how you would like to begin and end your presentation.

The Start

The introduction of a presentation must be very impactful. At the very beginning, it is important to draw the audience's attention and grow their eagerness towards your talk. As a presenter, try to build your credibility through the introduction and connect with your audience. Your presentation must start with a powerful introduction, the point at which you are going to explain the content and purpose of your presentation. This will form a crucial part of your talk as it is from this point that the audience's interest can be aroused.

Use any of the following strategies to prepare the introduction:

Make the introduction relevant to the objectives, values,

and needs of the audience.

- *Share a personal experience.*
- *Ask questions to stimulate thinking.*
- *Begin with a story.*
- *Project a visual or video*
- *Make a stimulating or inspirational statement.*
- *Give a unique demonstration.*

As you create your speech headline, make it like a one-sentence vision statement for your company, product, or service. Headlines that are specific and concise turn out to be the most effective. Begin with a catchy headline. Here is an example: Steve Jobs opened his presentation with:

"Welcome to Macworld 2008. There is something clearly in the air today." With those initial lines, Steve Jobs sets the theme for the big declaration of his keynote presentation— *The introduction of an ultrathin notebook computer.* He described it with the most apt words: *"MacBook Air. The world's thinnest notebook."*

Steve Jobs loved to create one-liners that best described his products. He not only created them as headlines but repeated them in the course of his presentation. As a presenter, create headlines in other words create taglines for your presentation and use them repeatedly to best describe the theme or the subject.

You may begin with a persuasive story that states a problem or crisis. Introduce the audience to the problem that needs to be resolved by the end of your presentation.

Establish the problem before giving out the solution. Describe your problem and show the pain it causes. You can best structure this through a storytelling device. Stories and questions are powerful tools to begin a presentation. Emphasise the question: "*What problem did I solve?*" In fact, this increases the possibility that the audience will connect with the speaker, understand the issue, and listen intently to him. Use stories to keep the audience engaged by making them expect closure. Where numbers list and facts merely inform and are mostly forgotten, storytelling has the power to make the audience understand with clarity, act on the information that is being presented, and remember the presentation for a long time.

Narrate a Story

In fact, storytelling is one of the best ways to captivate the audience's attention. Stories are much more engaging and memorable than dry facts and figures. Think of your presentation as a narrative. As mentioned earlier, structure it with a clear beginning, middle, and end. Use conflict in your narrative and provide a powerful resolution that will establish your key messages. For example, if the topic is on the benefits of health, the presenter may present a story or a study about how an individual's quality of life has significantly improved by following certain principles, exercises, and diet. Different case studies could also be added to help the audience connect better to such presentations. The audience is more likely to remember a story than a list of facts. I would cite another instance of Steve Jobs referring to the personal stories he used in his famous speech presentation (this one is available on the Stanford website). Steve Jobs began with a powerful opening and then moved on to his personal anecdotes, *"The first story is about connecting the dots."* After narrating this story, he says, *"My second story is about love and loss."* And the third story opens with, *"My third story is about death."* It is these stories that made his presentation memorable and unique. And he ends his presentation with the key message, *"Stay hungry, stay foolish."*

Use Appropriate Humour

Some of the best speeches and presentations feature plenty of humour. A good speaker will use humour to convey his points, lighten the mood of the audience and hold their attention towards the subject presented. Humour is an excellent way to connect with the audience. More experienced and confident public speakers start a presentation with a joke. A humour or a joke could be only used if the presenter is confident with this technique and has been successful in the past.

Start With a Video

Yet another strong and engaging way to start a presentation would be to show a one-minute pre-prepared video that can provide a great opening and draw the attention of the audience before they hear your speech. Choose a short video clip that better conveys your story or topic than words. Include a link to a different website or embed the video directly into your presentation software. But do run a trial of the video prior to the day of the presentation and keep a ready backup on a USB in case you need it.

An Impactful Start

Research and extensive studies generally indicate that since time is limited in a presentation, an impressive opening can indeed create a positive impact. What is important is to draw the attention of the audience with a strong and effective introduction that must come naturally with practice. An introduction to a presentation can then be delivered with confidence, passion, energy, and enthusiasm.

The key points form the backbone of the presenter's talk. These points play an important role in helping the presenter to prioritise, focus and sequence the information. When planning a presentation, put aside all research notes and prepare a summary of the main points. That would be helpful in answering questions like: *What exactly am I conveying to my audience? What would this presentation teach them?* The responses to these questions will help to convey clear, effective messages to the audience.

Finding a suitable headline is the next step. Headlines not only grab the attention of the audience but also give people a reason to listen. Another important thing is the passion for the subject. According to Aristotle, the Greek philosopher, successful speakers must have 'pathos' or passion for the subject. Therefore, once your headline is ready, look for a passion statement and write out three or four messages so that the audience will remember messages they will be able to recall in the future.

Speech Introduction Goals

The opening strategy you want to employ to captivate the audience should be carefully planned out as you prepare your introduction. The purpose of a good introduction is to achieve three goals:

- *Grasp the audience's attention.*

- *Identify the topic and the purpose or core message of the talk.*

- *Provide a brief overview of all that will be covered in the talk.*

Speech Openers in A Presentation

A presenter may begin a presentation by saying,

"A very good morning to all present here. I heartily welcome you all to my presentation…First of all, let me thank you for being here today." "My name is…let me start by saying a few words about my background…" or "Today I'm going to tell you a story…"

Quote Someone Else: A presenter may use a quote by someone else that helps set up what the talk is all about. When using a quote, cite the source of the line and tie the quote to your topic.

Share A Personal Experience: A short personal anecdote is another clever way to kick off your presentation. The story you share needs to contain a message that you can tie to the talk you will present.

Give An Interesting Example: In this technique, it is best to start with a case study or demonstration, showing something or describing a situation that illustrates the topic and its core message. To be effective, the example must be relevant and fairly brief.

An Example to Use in A Presentation

Present a Case Study: Describe a patient scenario.

Present the complication or problem.

Present statistics—recovery, deaths, or risk factors.

Present a solution and a call to action.

You could also start off with any of the following introductory statements:

- After greeting the audience with an introduction: a presenter may continue by stating what will be discussed: *"Today, I am going to explore ..." or "In my presentation, I will focus on three major issues..."*

- A statement of the principles to be applied to the topic (e.g., to compare, contrast, evaluate, describe): *"I will present before you the functions of... or I will be comparing the three main principles of ..." or "I am going to take a look at the recent developments in..."*

- A statement of what could be the outcome of a presentation: *"I hope this will provide us with a fair idea of ..."*

- A description of what the audience will need to do, such as when they can ask questions or if they need to take notes: The presenter might even say, *"I will pass around a handout that summarises my presentation before taking questions at the end."*

Transitions

Transitions are signposts that will help the audience to navigate through a presentation. They help divide information into sections, and sub-sections, link different aspects of your talk, and show the progression of the presented topic. Transitions draw the audience's attention by connecting the steps of the presentation as well as its content. Examples include:

- *"I will begin my presentation by exploring ...."*

- *"Now that we have discussed the ... I would like to move on to ...."*

- *"In contrast to the earlier part of my presentation concerning ...."*

Transitions can also be made without speaking. Non-verbal transitions include pausing, changing a slide or other visual aid, or making eye contact with a different group in the audience.

ENDING A PRESENTATION TALK

The Conclusion

The conclusion will establish how a problem has been dealt with, how it could be solved, or whether the need is satisfied. In other words, the solution should match and meet the challenges that emerged. At this point, you can summarise the talk's content and purpose, provide an overview of what has been accomplished, and leave a lasting impression.

While concluding a presentation, as a presenter, reinforce the main ideas communicated. It must be remembered that listeners will not remember an entire presentation, only the main ideas. Reinforcing and reviewing the main ideas helps the audience remember the key message. The conclusion could be similar to the options given below:

- A review of the topic and purpose of your presentation: *"In this presentation, I wanted to bring forth before you ..."*

- A statement of the conclusions or recommendations to be drawn from your work: *"I hope I have been able to show that the effects of ...."*

- An indication of the next stages (what might be done to take this work further?): *"At the end, I would like to wrap up by saying that this presentation does highlight the need for further research in the area of ...."*

- Instruction as to what happens next (questions, discussion, or group work?): *"I would now like to take the opportunity of answering your questions ...."*

- A sincere thanks to the audience for their participation and attention: *"That is all from my end. Thank you very much for your attention."*

Try to address the audience directly in your conclusion, just as you did in your introduction, to give the impression of a confident and useful speaker. It is odd when presenters include a concluding slide with just one or two words that either reads "Questions?" or "Thank You!" In most cases, audiences are not afraid to ask questions. As for thanking people, the best thing would be to thank people for their time and attention, either at the beginning or at the end of your presentation.

4

DELIVERY CONTENT & STYLE

It is time now to concentrate on the delivery style and content of your presentation. While delivering a presentation, keep in mind the different types of learners that will be part of the audience:

Visual learners

Auditory learners

A large percentage of the audience are 'visual' learners; they learn by seeing. For visual learners, avoid cluttering your slides with too much text. Prepare slides with fewer words and more pictures. Visual learners connect with what they see.

Another percentage of the audience is 'auditory' learners; they learn through listening. This section of the audience will connect with the stories and anecdotes they listen to in the course of your presentation.

There is yet another section of people who are

'kinesthetic' learners; they learn by doing, moving, etc. They are the ones who can be engaged in activities such as quizzes, exercises, polls, and surveys in the course of a presentation. Polls are similar to quizzes and engage the audience during a presentation. Polls encourage the audience to think about the questions and the possible answers. Live polls help to create mental breaks so that the audience can regain attention and stay focused on your presentation. *Questions will not only engage the audience but make them expect an answer. Ask the audience questions at the very start.*

As a presenter, cater to every type of learner in the audience, visual, auditory, and kinesthetic. Use your voice to share stories and anecdotes, limit the text on the slide to a bare minimum, use relevant images and pictures, and include exercises and activities such as polls and quizzes in your presentation.

Now, focus on the content and the essential supporting structure of your presentation. The building block of a presentation, the content, is the driving force behind an outstanding PowerPoint presentation. The importance of getting the presentation content right cannot be overstated. There is one thing, one theme, that you would want the audience to take away. It is what the audience will remember once the presentation is over. They will forget many of the details but will remember the key message. It is what will fire peoples' imaginations and what will motivate them to take action.

While writing the draft of the presentation script, focus on three things: language, structure, and the audience. Your ability to engage the audience is largely influenced by your choice of language. It is important to use language your audience understands and is familiar with. Transform your presentation into a visual story supported by the clarity of language, words, and slides.

It is best to avoid using language that is too formal or informal, too technical, or too simplistic. Depending on the nature of your talk and the knowledge base of your audience, create your content. Although it could be somewhat difficult to pitch your presentation at the right level, it is nevertheless very effective for getting the audience involved. To quote Leonardo da Vinci: *"Simplicity is the ultimate sophistication."* Your slides will stand out if they are simple. And there must be simplicity in the words you choose to deliver your presentation. Use simple, direct language that is free from any kind of jargon. The content delivered in simple, understandable English presented in a lucid style would be more acceptable than complex, difficult English. The complexity of a presentation is usually caused by the use of bombastic abstract words, technical jargon, and lack of a proper structure in communication.

Here are some important points to consider to effectively deliver the presentation:

Dress Appropriately for The Culture

Dress smartly and professionally for a presentation, depending on the content, formality of the occasion, and the type of audience.

Reach Your Presentation Venue Early

Arrive early for the presentation so that you are familiar with the logistics.

Decide How to Handle Audience Questions

Decide how you will take questions during the presentation; you can either opt for answering questions at the end or in the middle of your presentation.

Have A Plan If the Technology Fails

Similarly, decide how you will continue your presentation in case technology fails in the middle.

The Language of The Presentation

When it comes to the language of your presentation, clarity is of paramount importance. The delivered speech must be clear and concise, with each point following from the previous one. If you are narrating a story, narrate the story in the most comprehensible style. You do want people to understand, absorb and remember, so use words that are understandable and keep your word choice simple. The audience would not look up a dictionary for every difficult word they come across in a presentation. To keep the audience engaged, the presenter has to express complex ideas in short, simple sentences and be straight and to the point.

Talk In 'Conversational' Style, Not In 'Formal Written English' Style

The style of delivery should be interactive and conversational, quite different from that of written English. If you are preparing your presentation script, remember to change your delivery style from written ornamental to spoken conversational. However, to use a conversational style and be natural would require a lot of practice. Give yourself enough time to rehearse your presentation. Do not forget to pay attention to how your slides will complement your speech. Check your timings; remember that adequate practice will turn you into a confident presenter.

Different Ways of Delivering Your Presentation

A remarkably interesting way of presenting is through stories. Audiences love content that is presented in the form of a story supported by facts and figures. The presenter should try not to bore the audience with spreadsheets full of data. Dry statistics do not resonate with people unless they understand the context. Too many numbers overwhelm the audience. Alternately put them in the form of a short, interesting story. This will bring credibility to the presentation content and the speaker.

To bring credibility to your content, quote great personalities and draw examples from the lives of prominent leaders. Opening with a quotation can reaffirm the validity of an argument, launch an idea, and strengthen it. Steve Jobs kept his content simple and full of emotive language, which meant that his audience understood and related to him, and this allowed him to establish not only the credibility of his message but also kept his audience awestruck. Jobs loved to sell 'dreams' to his audience. Such extraordinary were his presentations.

5

HOW TO USE STORIES & SCRIPTS

A presentation topic can best be backed by a story from a real-life case study or survey. Stories create wonders in a presentation. A story will give you the confidence and power to win over an audience. Humans have been telling stories since time immemorial. We all connect to stories. Researchers have revealed that humans think in terms of a story incredibly early in life. A major reason for using stories in presentations is, therefore, to convey a message that will be remembered for a very long time. Stories are memorable. Stories can explain complex messages in simple words. It is, therefore, never difficult to understand a story in order to explain a complex message. But stories need to have clarity.

Let us figure out how we can use stories in a presentation. Going by Aristotle's classic five-point plan, we can divide a story for a presentation into five parts.

1. Create a **STORY** that arouses the audience's interest.

2. Raise a **PROBLEM** that has to be solved or

answered.

3. Offer a **SOLUTION** to the problem raised.

4. Describe the **BENEFITS** of adopting the course of action.

5. State a call to **ACTION**. What do you want your audience to do?

Script your ideas in a notepad or on paper. Visualise the story and keep it simple. Create a story that interests the audience. As Cliff Atkinson points out, *"The single most important thing you can do to dramatically improve your presentations is to have a story to tell before you work on your PowerPoint file."*

Atkinson suggests a three-step process:

According to Cliff Atkinson, it is only after writing down the script, could a presenter think visually about how the slides will look. He suggests that *"You need to set aside PowerPoint design issues like font, colours, backgrounds and slide transitions...when you write a script first, you actually expand your visual possibilities, because writing defines your purpose before you start designing." "A script unlocks the undiscovered power of PowerPoint as a visual story-telling tool in ways that might surprise and delight you and your audience."* Your ideas must be scripted at the very beginning. A PowerPoint presentation without a written structure is like planning a film without a script. The narrative needs to be written down first before designing the slides. The narrative can captivate the minds of the audience. The script of the presentation story is, therefore, of utmost importance.

A story planned for a presentation is first sketched on paper and later transferred into ideas for slides. Creating the plot of a story is the first step in presenting ideas successfully. Effective communicators plan every step of their narrative through compelling passages, persuasive headlines, and effective slides, making it easier for the audience to understand the core message.

Following Aristotle's classical elements of storytelling, a presentation story must therefore have a beginning, a middle, and an end. Based on these three sections or parts, a presenter could begin the first part of the story by introducing the key elements, the setting, the main character, the conflict, and the desired outcome. The second or middle part can take the story forward by picking up on the conflict and developing it through a variety of conditions. The third or end part creates a climax, and a decision to resolve the conflict, the benefits of adopting a certain course of action, and a call to action, i.e., what the audience is expected to do. Presenting stories, anecdotes, and case studies are some of the best ways to engage and entertain the audience.

A story will help focus on an idea and bind together all the loose pieces of information. You not only need to inform but also persuade the audience through your stories. Stories are important in all kinds of communication because they arouse interest. You need not be an expert storyteller to use a story in your presentation. Just keep in mind that your story must persuade the audience to focus on your key message, it must arouse their interest through verbal and visual clarity, and it must help them understand the problem presented and how to bring about a possible solution. Your narrative, complemented with a visually engaging presentation, will enthral your audience.

Some presenters apply the **SPA** method while telling stories. SPA stands for **Story**, **Point**, and **Application**. The STORY must have a POINT and an APPLICATION. There is no use telling a story just for the sake of it. The point must be related to the topic and must apply to the audience. There is a saying, *'Never tell a story without a point and never make a point without a story.'*

There are actually many benefits of storytelling. Stories are mostly original. Audiences are eager to hear what comes next in the story. In fact, stories can even make familiar information fresh and interesting. An interactive presentation could encourage audiences to add to a story their own mental images of the setting and the characters. This explains why some people can remember stories weeks after a presentation.

Stories To Solve a Problem

Begin your presentation by providing a context of a story related to the topic presented and introducing the main characters. Remember, the audience needs to connect to your story. They should be able to empathise or sympathise with the characters. As you move to the next part of a story, discuss the problem that would keep the audience engaged. Begin with the background of a problem, how the problem has grown, how you may find a solution, and how it has affected people's lives. A good story should have a solution that is logical and feasible. If you want the audience to remember your key points, the best practice is to package the key points with a short story or anecdote. A marketing executive from a pharmaceutical company was once giving a presentation on their top-selling product before a fairly large audience. He included a case study in his presentation where he showed a photo of a woman in a wheelchair with rheumatoid arthritis. He mentioned the drug was particularly indicated for her problem. He then showed the photo of the same woman walking after six months of treatment. Stories like this make your presentation interesting. Use both emotion and logic to make a story memorable. The audience will hear the story, visualise it, and remember it.

Stories From Statistics and Data

There is yet another kind of story—the story of data. How do you put data into a story? You need to provide a context on the basis of the data provided below on a topic of the presentation, say, for example, *Child labour*.

Facts From Different Resources:

1. *There are 160 million children engaged in child labour in the world today, accounting for nearly 10 per cent of the world's children. Since 2016, the*

number of children engaged in child labour has increased from 8.4 million to 160 million. That amounts to 97 million boys and 63 million girls.

2. *Children all over the world regularly engage in non-harmful forms of paid and unpaid work. However, when they are either too young to work or are involved in hazardous activities that may compromise their physical, mental, social, or educational development, they are considered child labourers. In many under-developed countries, one in four children (ages 5 to 17 years) are engaged in labour that is considered detrimental to their health and growth.*

3. *One-fifth of the world's children are engaged in child labour, and Africa has the highest total number of children in child labour—72 million. Asia and the Pacific come in the second place, with 62 million children working as child labour in this region.*

4. *According to the study from the International Labour Organization (ILO) and UNICEF, Child Labour: Global Estimates 2020 shows a sharp rise in children aged 5 to 11 years being forced to work and pushed into jobs that are extremely harmful to them.*

5. *News on Child Labour from Cocoa farms:*

In a recent article published in April 2022, the headline in leading newspapers read, "Cadbury faces fresh accusations of child labour on cocoa farms in Ghana." There is a fresh allegation brought against Mondelēz International, which owns Cadbury, of employing child labour. This comes after an investigation obtained footage of children working with machetes (a heavy knife) on cocoa farms in its supply chain. In Ghana, children as young as 10 years allegedly worked to harvest cocoa pods for Mondelz International. According to campaigners, farmers are paid less than £2 a day and cannot afford to hire adult workers. Therefore, they use child labour as a cheaper option. A film on the subject showed how children were made to use sharp knives to open cocoa pods and carried swinging long sticks with blades tied to them to harvest the pods from the cocoa trees. None of the children wore protective clothing. According to a report, a girl in child labour claimed to have sliced her foot open while using a long machete. Unfortunately, child labour continues 20 years after promises were made to completely eradicate it.

Projecting and presenting the above data and statistics could make a presentation on *Child Labour* very dull and monotonous. However, this presentation could come alive with some case studies or real-life stories on child labour. Here are examples of stories that could be a part of a presentation speech:

The Story as Part of a Presentation Speech:

I am going, to begin with a story of a young boy. Sam lived with her mother and two other siblings in great poverty in a village named Dago, in the eastern region of Ghana. One day Sam was abducted and taken away to a cocoa farm. A trafficker abducted him when he was just nine and sold it to the owner of a cocoa farm. Cocoa farms employ a huge number of child labourers. Sam was brought as a child labourer to one such cocoa farm in Ghana. Since then, he has been working there. The irony is that chocolate, a favourite food for children n worldwide, has cocoa as its main ingredient, produced from the cocoa grown in cocoa farms. Not having seen his family for years, Sam tried to run away once. However, as fate would have it, he was caught and so severely beaten up that he could not stand on his feet for days. Sam was not the only one. In fact, such children who had been trafficked could never go back to their families because traffickers sell them to work on cocoa farms for a certain number of years. According to recent statistics, more than 2.1 million children in the Ivory Coast and Ghana work on cocoa farms, most of who are exposed to the worst form of child labour. These children are between the ages of 12 and 16, but there have been reports that children as young as five years have also been brought to work here. Not only are these children deprived of the joys of a carefree childhood and their right to basic education, but they are also compelled to work as cheap labour in the worst possible conditions. Children under the age of 13 are prohibited from working on cocoa farms under Ghanaian law. There is also a ban on anyone under 18 being involved in hazardous labour, yet child labour continues. Instead of being eradicated, child labour remains a major concern for all, even in the 21st century.

Another Story Based on Child Labour

Here is another story of 9-year-old Rohan, who helps his mother collect rubbish, including old cans and plastic bottles, from a city street in Kolkata in the early morning hours to sell. At lunchtime, Rohan's mother would count her money. If the earning is more, she could afford to buy food and some eggs for her three children. If the money is less after selling the cans and bottles, she would have to manage with some bread for them.

Relevant Slides/Visuals on Child Labour That Could Complement the Stories:

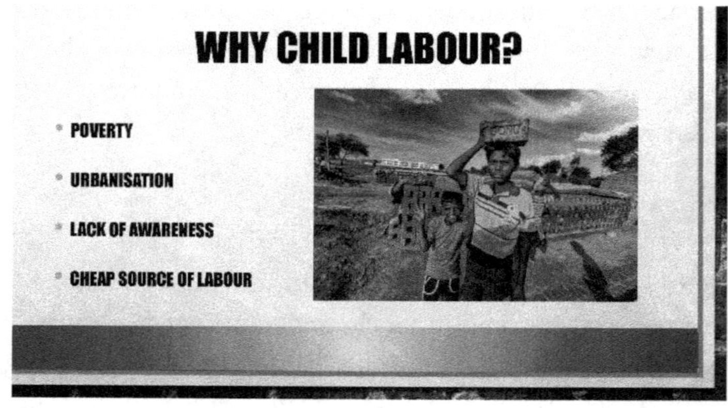

CHILD LABOUR — LATE 1700'S & EARLY 1900'S

CHILD LABOUR STORIES- IN COCOA FARMS

CHILD LABOUR — TWO CASE STUDIES

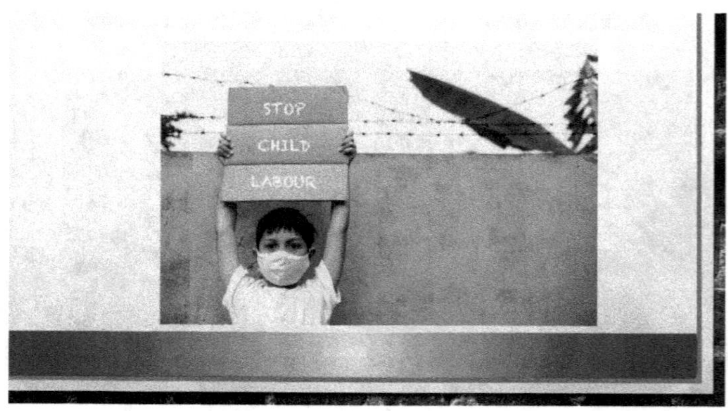

Such presentation of stories of Child labour could draw the attention of the audience and take them beyond dry statistics. These and similar stories would help the audience to connect to the topic presented. Stories narrated in a presentation would remain etched in the memory of the audience for an exceptionally long time to come. People may forget facts and figures mentioned in a presentation, but they do remember good stories. Narrating a true story is more powerful than a handful of data, analogies, or metaphors put together. Stories are real and have a great impact on the minds of people. Stories touch people's emotions.

Credibility of a Story:

The most effective presentations are made through credible stories. It is important to engage people's emotions while using stories as messages for presentation. But to create a story, just take a pen and paper in the planning phase, sketch the story, and prepare the script as well. You can later turn the sketches into slides. Do not create too many slides for a truly short presentation. For a 10-minute presentation, you need not create more than 5 slides.

Stories in the Middle of A Presentation Exemplify and Give Meaning to Key Points

Shorter and more concise stories used throughout a presentation (supported by an arresting image, relevant quote, or illuminating infographic) could effectively bring to life the core ideas that would be put forward before the audience. However, one must be careful not to use too many stories in the course of a presentation.

Use a Story/Video at the End to Provide One Last Inspiring Thought Before You Finish.

Video

A presentation could be effectively ended with a story, a relevant video clip, or a poetic quote that could serve as the perfect cherry on top of a proverbial cake. It would be an appropriate way to give the audience one last moment of connecting back and reinforcing the key messages. Very rarely do presenters incorporate videos in their presentations. Include a video clip of a minute or so in your presentation, and let it stand out from the rest.

How to Find Stories

Now from where do you find stories? There is really no limit to the sources that can yield a good story. Stories can come from just about anywhere: from personal experience or from the experiences shared by others, from books, newspapers and magazines, the internet, movies, and TV programs. Some presenters even look for stories in mythology. You can recycle and adapt stories others have already used. Just be sure your listeners are not likely to have heard the story before. However, if you do lift a story from somewhere, do give credit to the source.

6

DESIGNING SLIDES: LESS IS MORE

Creating PowerPoint Slides

What is Slide Design in a Presentation?

Presenters, most of the time, are obsessed with slides. The emphasis is too much on slide designing and preparing slides that are cluttered with too many ideas, words, and images, so much so that the audience slips into boredom with no curiosity left to hear the presenter.

The importance of visuals or pictures can never be denied. A picture is three times as effective in conveying information as words alone. Words and pictures taken together are six times as effective as words alone. A picture is the best method of conveying an idea. The visuals often are what remain in people's minds long after a presentation ends. Visuals help the audience remember facts and figures, understand ideas and information, and create an overall impact.

But slides are not stories. Slides will complement your speech and the stories that you share. Slides are visual aids

that will help the audience understand your message. You are the pivot of the presentation, not your slides. You are the presenter; you are the speaker, and it is for you to engage with the audience and present a clear message with or without slides. Slides should not be your crutch without which you cannot present. It is just an option you have used to enhance your presentation content. Therefore, take a three-step approach before you start designing your slides.

Start designing your slides only after you have structured the key message and script of your presentation. Use slides to complement your speech and arouse the interest of the audience. Keep your slides visually simple. Now, let us discuss how to create more emphasis with Slide Hierarchy. Slide hierarchy is placing the visual elements in a way that creates emphasis. Visual hierarchy is the order in which we create visual dominance of one element over the other. There are different ways in which this dominance could be created, such as using colours, contrast, spacing, typography, etc.

One Message Per Slide

The best practice is to have just one message per slide. You may be permitted to use some text on your slides, but the limitation for each slide is not more than five words across and five words down. *Sentences and paragraphs are not allowed on a visual PowerPoint slide.* As you present, remember to keep the slides as visual supports to demonstrate key points.

Avoid Background Templates

Most slide presentations are created on 'background' templates. But a template should not be a constraint for a presenter. A background template slide demands the inclusion of a slide title. Slide titles are useful, but there are times when no title is required, and the full screen is required to display more important things. To display large graphs or graphic elements, you should sometimes do without background templates. Templates restrict the workable area for graphs, diagrams, or images. For this, take a large white rectangle a little larger than the screen size. Then select the rectangle and apply the 'move to back' function. This will create a totally new slide not restricted by any form of template background.

PowerPoint slides should be able to convey the presenter's message to the audience in a proper sequence. To do so, first, decide what message you want to convey to the audience through presentation slides. And how exactly the audience could absorb the message. You could decide what you want the flow of a viewer's eyes to be.

Avoid Too Much Text

Placing all textual information on the slides results in slide clutter and information overload. Do not display too much text on the screen; the audience will read it and stop listening to you. Texts and Bullets in presentation slides are the least effective. When there is too much text on the screen, it reduces understanding. The audience tries to read the slides and pays little attention to the presenter. Redundancy takes place when the same information is presented both as images or pictures and in text form. Use your voice instead and limit the text on the slide to a bare minimum. Avoid bullet points, and if you do use them, make each bullet appear individually as you introduce it. Or introduce images as you talk about them. If you include some text, stick only to keywords, a date, a question, and elaborate and explain as you present. The audience will listen to you with rapt attention because you have aroused their curiosity by not letting out all of your slides.

Colour

Colours are the best for creating emphasis in presentations. Different colours evoke different kinds of emotions in the audience. For the purpose of business presentation, colours such as red, grey, and orange can be used. They represent dynamism, innovation, and maturity. For presentations on policies and regulation, teal, grey, and dark green looks more impressive.

Colours should be used to:

- Distinguish categories of different data in graphs.
- Distinguish values in a table.
- Highlight positive and negative results in different colours.

- Highlight warnings, important results in colour.

While creating slides with perfect colour combinations, contrast is vital. Each slide should have a sharp contrast between the background and foreground (text and graphics) so that they do not blend into each other and compromise legibility. This immediately classifies colour themes into two broad categories:

a) Dark Background—Light Foreground

b) Light Background—Dark Foreground

In the example below, notice how the parts with a darker background have the foreground of white text and icons and vice versa. Because of this, there is a contrast, making the foreground stand out from the background and not compete with it. The audience finds it difficult to read texts on slides that are not in sharp contrast (e.g., yellow on a white background or red on a blue background.)

BLACK	WHITE	RED
Mystery	Purity	Love
Power	Simplicity	Passion
Death	Goodness	Energy
Classy	Hope	Danger

YELLOW	GREY	GREEN
Friendliness	Authority	Life
Warmth	Maturity	Growth
Intellect	Stability	Nature
		Freshness

ORANGE	PURPLE	BLUE
Innovation	Royalty	Peace
Creativity	Dignity	Sincerity
	Wisdom	Tranquillity
		Integrity

However, keep in mind not to misuse colour. Too much colour leads to distraction. Let colour bring some benefit or else use only black and white.

Use Same Fonts

Most slide presentations are filled with texts in various font sizes (e.g., Verdana, Arial, or Cambria all appear on the same slide). It looks rather unprofessional and careless. Use fonts in a consistent manner and simple ones that are easy to read. Do not use fonts smaller than 18.

Overcome Ambiguity with Thoughtful Typography

Most presentations are based on words, so it is vital to realise which words to incorporate and how to style them.

This starts with choosing the right font and then knowing the font size and where to include them. Avoid using anything smaller in size than a 36-point font. Some presenters prefer to use sizes as small as 24-point font size, but this often leads to slide cluttering and visibility issues.

Here are a few principles that you need to keep in mind while creating effective power point slides:

1. Use Short Texts with Key Ideas and Relevant Images

The most important principle is to consider the outcome if you bring before the audience slides full of texts and simultaneously speak as you present. The audience will remember almost nothing of what you have said or delivered. Replace the longer texts you thought of including in your slides with short important bits of text and a relevant image. This will enhance your message. A presentation of this simplicity tells the audience to pay closer attention to what the speaker is saying.

2. Reverse the Font Size for Title & Content

We always look at the headline or the title of a slide first because the fonts are bigger and bolder in comparison to the content. Even readymade power point templates have the headline in a bigger font and the contents in smaller fonts. But is the headline always the most important part of a power point slide? Is it not the content of a slide that conveys the actual message? If you reduce the title size and use bigger fonts for the content, you will be able to draw the attention of the audience towards the content.

3. Highlight Important Points

Highlight the area you want the audience to concentrate on. For example, while elaborating on the first point, highlight it, then move to the second point and highlight it again, then the third and so on.

The Screen Ratio

It is important to use the right screen ratio. Most projectors use the 16:9 ratio. But some people use the old 4:3. The result is two black columns on each side, thereby losing the opportunity to utilise the useful spaces on either side. If you are switching an existing 4:3 slide to a 16:9 slide, some fixing is required, or else both the text and images get distorted.

Animations

Animations are necessary for visual cues to appear at the right time when the speaker is talking about them. When animating, use only two types of animation 'appear' and 'disappear'. Avoid all kinds of fancy animations, such as flying over the screen…this may be annoying and distracting for the audience. It is also good to avoid transitions in-between slides.

Now, before planning the slides, remember not to make the slides look monotonous and hackneyed. We have experiences of sitting through innumerable presentations where slides have been cluttered with texts, graphics, and images, all in one. Not all visuals enhance a presentation. The use of too many cluttered slides disinterests the audience, turns them off, and puts them to sleep. With too many irrelevant slides, the audience might experience the oft-repeated phrase '*Death by PowerPoint*'.

The following types of visuals could be very disappointing for the audience and should be avoided:

a) Too many slides

b) Cluttering each slide with dense text and many images

c) Complex, confusing visuals, such as flow charts, graphs, boxes, arrows, loops, text

d) Simply reading the text from the visuals aloud

For compelling, effective visuals in your presentation:

a) Keep slides simple.

b) Use keywords, not full sentences.

c) Only one idea per slide

d)   Use contrasting colours.

e)   Pictures, if feasible.

f)   Avoid all forms of visual clutter.

With Slides, Less is More.

It is true that most successful professionals do not need too many slides to present. A six-minute presentation could even do without any slides. In short, you probably need fewer slides than you think. If your slides contain too much information, the audience will divert from listening to a mode where they can simply skim through your slides.

Presentations with PowerPoint have become the easiest tool that could be used in every field of work. However, most presentations fall flat in the face if the audience reads from the slides without paying much attention to what the presenter has to say. In other words, slides that are overloaded with information and cluttered with text have nothing left for the audience to anticipate or guess. In such instances, the curiosity of the audience is lost as they monotonously stare at the slide texts, waiting for yet another presentation to get over.

The presentation itself is not exceedingly difficult to master. But most people are caught up using PowerPoint, forgetting what it is actually for. Once the presentation content is narrowed and the key message is clear, the speaker can include the accessories in the form of slide visuals that will help the audience retain what they have learned.

A variety of visuals could be included in the form of:

a) Photos or other images

b) Charts or graphs

c) Maps

d) Video clips

e) Handouts (only when necessary—they can be distracting)

Communicate through Graphic Simplicity

The target should always be to make visuals simple but compelling and impactful in a presentation. Include appropriate graphics, icons, and symbols to explain various concepts. Every chart, graph, icon, illustration, or photograph used in a presentation should be easy to see and understand. Suitable graphics, charts, pictures, diagrams, and even videos (check copyright issues) could be inserted in the slides to support your presentation. In the slide below, an example of a hierarchical structure of the School of Engineering in a university is presented:

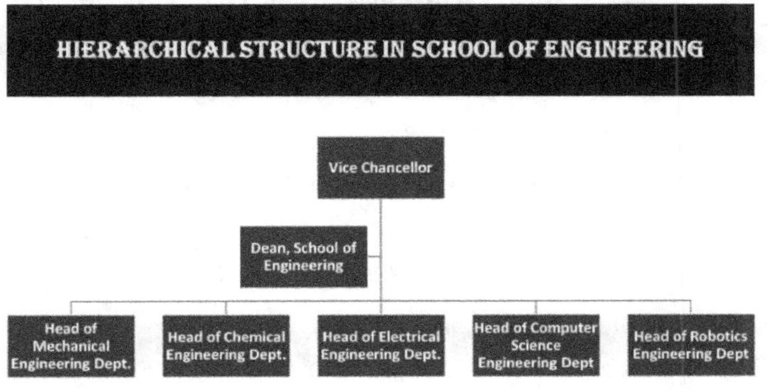

Audience trust can be eroded by images that are unclear or of poor quality. Symbols, icons, or illustrations should be used in a way to communicate ideas faster than photography. Another important point is to use keywords instead of full sentences. Precision is the key to all successful presentations.

Here is a summary of the basic rules that must be followed while designing visuals.

- *Use a simple, neutral background. A light-coloured background with fonts in a dark colour or a dark background with contrasting photos will stand out. Make sure the fonts are large enough for the audience to read.*

- *It is important to minimise the amount of text in visuals. Use images to support your presentation; never use clip art just for decoration.*

- *Avoid putting a table of numbers in a visual aid. If you need to illustrate numerical data, use a graph instead.*

- *Refrain from using sound effects and visual special effects such as dissolves, spins, box-outs, or other forms of transitions. The audience will find them distracting. Use animation sparingly and only if it helps make a point.*

- *Do not use too many visuals or move through them so fast that the audience gives all its attention to them rather than to what you are saying.*

- *Practice your presentation using your visual aids because they will affect your timing.*

- *Make eye contact with the audience, briefly glancing at the relevant slides.*

- *Do not put your entire script or large chunks of text in the slides.*

- *Do not read from the slides as you present.*

- *Use slides for what they are: visual aids. Include relevant pictures, if needed. Use them to highlight ideas, words, or concepts.*

- *Email yourself a copy of the presentation, if possible, in case there is a problem with your flash drive, the USB port, or other technical difficulties.*

- *Use standard fonts.*

- *If technical difficulties are irresolvable, it is best to be prepared to give a presentation without a slideshow. Your slides are not your presentation; just support it.*

There are two key aspects to focus on improving: you and your slides. Your slides should function as a roadmap, helping you and your audience to follow the main ideas. Here is how to build a great roadmap.

- **Focus on one idea at a time.**

- **Introduce a single point on a slide.**

- **Do not write paragraphs.**

For the written word, a presentation is not an appropriate platform. Do not introduce a paragraph on a slide and read it aloud; people can read faster in their heads than you can on stage. So, stick to a minimal amount of text usage and never read out from the slides.

Paint A Bigger Picture

It is nice to have a summary slide at the end of the talk that captures your key ideas. However, most of those concepts will be lost to the audience after a few days. What would be the one thing you want them to remember? Place your work in a larger context. People are more likely to remember the bigger picture than the minute details of your work.

Slide Designing and Content for a Short Presentation on 'Anxiety':

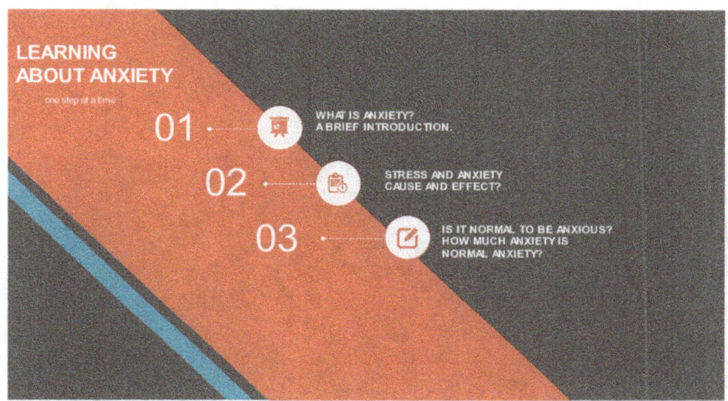

LEARNING
ABOUT ANXIETY
one step at a time
01
WHAT IS ANXIETY?
A BRIEF INTRODUCTION.
02
STRESS AND ANXIETY
CAUSE AND EFFECT?
03
IS IT NORMAL TO BE ANXIOUS?
HOW MUCH ANXIETY IS
NORMAL ANXIETY?

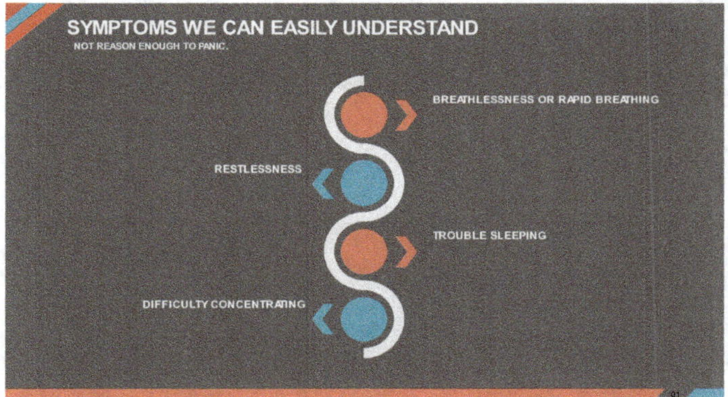

SYMPTOMS WE CAN EASILY UNDERSTAND
NOT REASON ENOUGH TO PANIC.
BREATHLESSNESS OR RAPID BREATHING
RESTLESSNESS
TROUBLE SLEEPING
DIFFICULTY CONCENTRATING

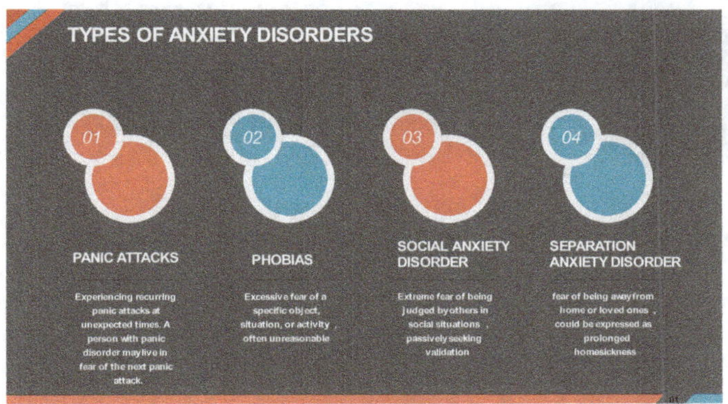

TYPES OF ANXIETY DISORDERS
01
02
03
04
PANIC ATTACKS
PHOBIAS
SOCIAL ANXIETY
DISORDER
SEPARATION
ANXIETY DISORDER
Experiencing recurring
panic attacks at
unexpected times. A
person with panic
disorder may live in
fear of the next panic
attack.
Excessive fear of a
specific object,
situation, or activity ,
often unreasonable
Extreme fear of being
judged by others in
social situations ,
passively seeking
validation
fear of being away from
home or loved ones ,
could be expressed as
prolonged
homesickness

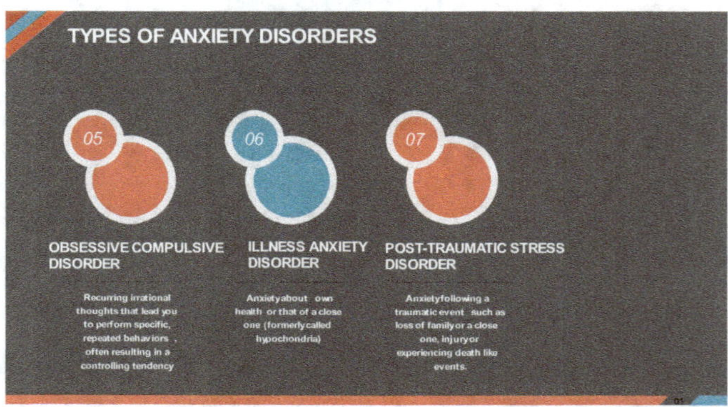
TYPES OF ANXIETY DISORDERS
05
06
07
OBSESSIVE COMPULSIVE DISORDER
ILLNESS ANXIETY DISORDER
POST-TRAUMATIC STRESS DISORDER
Recurring irrational thoughts that lead you to perform specific, repeated behaviors, often resulting in a controlling tendency
Anxiety about own health or that of a close one (formerly called hypochondria)
Anxiety following a traumatic event such as loss of family or a close one, injury or experiencing death like events.

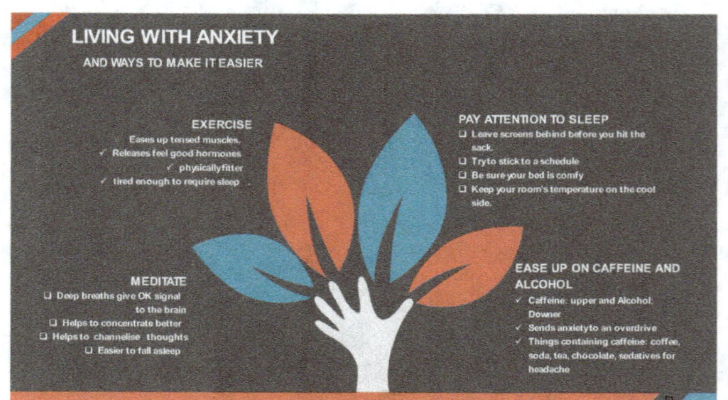
LIVING WITH ANXIETY
AND WAYS TO MAKE IT EASIER
EXERCISE
Eases up tensed muscles.
Releases feel good hormones
physically fitter
tired enough to require sleep
PAY ATTENTION TO SLEEP
Leave screens behind before you hit the sack.
Try to stick to a schedule
Be sure your bed is comfy
Keep your room's temperature on the cool side.
MEDITATE
Deep breaths give OK signal to the brain
Helps to concentrate better
Helps to channelise thoughts
Easier to fall asleep
EASE UP ON CAFFEINE AND ALCOHOL
Caffeine: upper and Alcohol: Downer
Sends anxiety to an overdrive
Things containing caffeine: coffee, soda, tea, chocolate, sedatives for headache

7

MINIMAL USE OF TECHNOLOGY

Technologies, when used ineffectively in a presentation, can take the focus away from the speaker. Your message is most likely to get lost with the excessive use of technology. Illustrate your key messages with personal stories or real case studies. The more personal and emotional your stories are, the more successful you will be with your presentation. Many of the best TED speakers prefer not to even use slides in their talks. If photographs or illustrations can make a topic come alive, then it is good to use them as support for the talk. Try to give some parts of your presentation without visuals.

Slides can help frame and pace a talk and help speakers avoid getting lost in jargon or overly intellectual language. A common technology used by some presenters is to put slides on an automatic timer so that the image changes every 15 seconds. However, it is always better to turn off the automatic timer and change slides manually according to the progress of the accompanied talk. Another impactful way is when a presenter gives a talk accompanied by a video, speaking along to it. That creates an altogether different experience for the audience.

Here are some common technical glitches that most presenters encounter and must be ready to handle. For instance, if your presentation was created in PowerPoint 2016 and you need to use the system with a slightly older version (e.g., Office 2013) at the venue, your content might get messed up. Not to mention PPTX files from newer versions sometimes simply fail to open with older versions. The remedy for that can be to save the file as a PPT to run it in compatibility mode. But in spite of that, your presentation can lag because of conversion, and some animations and transitions available for newer versions may not run in the older version. Needless to say, using your own computer might be a safer option. Therefore, it is best to use your own laptop, accounts for connectivity cables and drivers, and test-run your slides prior to the presentation. On the contrary, if you are going to use something like a phablet, make sure you remove the sim. The last thing you want is a caller ID replacing your on-screen slides when you get a phone call in the middle of your presentation.

Most of the serious problems we see at presentations and conferences happen when presenters try to include audio and video content in their presentations. Simple slide shows are usually trouble-free, but the use of multimedia may lead to technical and non-technical trouble.

The amount of time required to actually use a video or audio in a presentation is frequently overlooked by presenters. It may be a 30-second clip, but setting it up, talking about it, and explaining it, takes a much longer time than expected.

You might want to record, or video record your presentation or ask a friend or roommate to watch your presentation. Pay attention to the aspects of how you speak:

- *Try to speak in a natural voice, not in a monotone, as if you were just reading aloud. If you will be presenting in a large room without a microphone, you will need to speak louder than usual but still try to use a natural voice.*

- *Be certain you can articulate every new word and specialised term accurately. Practice saying them to yourself slowly and clearly until you are able to say them naturally.*

- *Do not forget transitions. As you shift to a new idea, audience members require a prompt. Practice expressions, for example, "Another important reason for this is…" or "Now let's move on to why this is so.…"*

- *Keep an eye out for all of the frequently used "filler" words, such as "like," "you know," "well," and "uh." The majority of viewers find them very distracting. To determine whether you are using these fillers, check your recording, watch it, or ask a friend to point it out.*

- *Finally, it is a good idea to be ready in case of an accident. Most likely, your presentation will go smoothly, you will be on track with your notes, and your PowerPoint slides will work fine, but sometimes mishaps do happen.*

If the computer fails and you lose your visuals, be ready for any form of technical glitch and carry photos and handouts to share with the audience. If your presentation faces a technical glitch, acknowledge it with a smile and carry on. Keep the larger picture in mind, enjoy, add humour, and do not pay attention to the trifles. After all, your presentation is a piece of infotainment where the audience wants not only to be informed but entertained too.

If you have incorporated media files into your presentation, be careful that while PowerPoint embeds images into the PowerPoint presentation file, it frequently only 'links' to audio and video files and does not embed them. This means that if you move a copy of your PowerPoint presentation to a different computer but do not move the media files the same way, the video, sounds, and other multimedia content will not show up when you try to show them. The best solution to this is to put all the relevant media files and the PowerPoint master file in the same folder (do this while building a presentation so that you add the media files into the shared folder) and then insert them into the presentation.

There may be additional complications because not all computers are capable of playing all media formats. This is especially true when transferring files from Macs to PCs or the other way around.

Please do not assume that any computer can play any given media format, even when the video is embedded in a PowerPoint video, and you are playing it on PowerPoint for Mac. Therefore, test and run all audio, sound, and other files before the final presentation. You can opt for adding videos from online sources. Many presentation apps, like PowerPoint, Prezi, Google Slides, etc., do allow embedding online videos.

The first rule of internet use for presentations is to possibly avoid connecting to the internet while presenting. In some cases, be that as it may, there is no viable alternative to the web. You might be demonstrating a website or web-based application. In that case, you need to have a backup plan if you lose connectivity, or something does not seem to work properly and test it beforehand on the presentation computer in the location you plan to connect to the network you plan to use.

There is a story of how once the internet failed during a presentation, Steve Jobs and the Apple team did not panic. Jobs shared a story from the past, and in the meantime, the tech support team fixed the problem. This is a good strategy to keep the audience engaged and entertained while someone fixes the problem. Always be prepared for similar situations. You need to ensure that you keep a backup of your whole presentation, with media files, on a portable drive. If the presentation, sound, video, or computer suddenly fails, or you run into a compatibility issue, be ready to switch to another machine like a real 'pro'. It is always wise to back up your presentation to the Cloud using OneDrive, iCloud, or Google Drive. This will provide you with an instant backup for your presentation in case of any eventuality but also give you a PowerPoint alternative in case you need one.

This is how you can make a presentation effective with the minimal use of technology:

- *Keeping it simple.*
- *Creating a compelling structure—organise your presentation in proper order.*

- *Giving a narrative to your presentation—telling a story—sharing an event from your life or an anecdote that will connect you to the audience.*

- *Use visual aids but do not clutter your slides.*

- *Avoiding chunks of text on a single slide.*

- *Showing only main points or relevant images on the screen—then explaining them in detail.*

- *Smiling and making eye contact with the audience.*

- *Working on your stage presence and body language.*

- *Starting strong with an introduction that draws the target audience.*

- *Bringing passion to your presentation.*

- *Breathing—say all that you want to convey to the audience, but do not rush through your presentation.*

- *Practising hard.*

A talk could be presented with or without visuals. The most memorable talks offer something fresh, something no one has heard before. The worst ones are the ones that follow some kind of formula and sound very clichéd. And in case technology fails completely, you may rely on your natural charm and wit to hold the audience's attention. Prepare and keep ready your backup materials for worst-case scenarios. The idea is to make the talk your very own. You know what is distinctive about you and your ideas. Play to your strengths and give a talk that reflects your authenticity. The biggest decision in your presentation talk is to figure out where and how to start and where and how to end.

8

AUDIENCE BEFORE CONTENT

In this chapter, we are going to discuss the importance of an audience in a presentation. Most presenters make the mistake of not thinking about the target audience. We write scripts and compile our talking points, but we do not think about our audience and what they need or expect to get out of our presentation. This has serious consequences. If the audience feels your words do not apply to them, or they do not understand what you are trying to say, or, worse, they do not care about your ideas, then your well-crafted slides, your talk, or even your jokes simply do not matter.

Speakers need to practice their ABCs: Audience Before Content First.

The implication captures the essence of what your presentation is all about—it is not about you, the speaker; it is always about your audience. The need of the audience must be the focus of your attention. It is important to know your audience so you can pitch your presentation well. Planning your presentation around your target audience is a smart move. Your task is to impart information to the audience that they are unlikely to know. Think about how much they know about the subject and why they are listening to your presentation.

Presentation expert Clif Atkinson tells a great story about a 2009 education conference where two speakers got quite different reactions from their audiences. The first speaker started off with interactive exercises, he was entertaining, and overall, his presentation was a hit and hugely liked by his audience. The second speaker chose to use a more traditional PowerPoint, and his presentation did not go quite well with the audience. In fact, while he presented, bored attendees even started a "backchannel" on Twitter. They critiqued his slides, content, and his delivery.

Three Things to Know About Your Audience

Prior to preparing your speech, you should gather the following three essential pieces of information about your audience:

1. Why would the audience be interested in your topic?

You must comprehend why your topic is significant to your audience in order to connect with them. What do they expect to learn from the presentation? Don't assume the audience is like you. They may have cultural or geographic biases—and the more you understand those biases, the better you can express your ideas and avoid blunders in speaking.

2. The level of knowledge your audience has about the topic.

Comprehend how much your listeners are familiar with the subject so you can present your data using the right tone to keep them intrigued and locked in. Presenting basic information to a highly knowledgeable audience or speaking at a level that is too high for a novice audience is never a good idea.

3. Cultural differences your audience may have.

If you are presenting in a foreign country, it is important for you to understand the cultural differences of the audience. How do they dress? How is their sense of humour? How do they typically communicate? What gestures are appropriate or inappropriate? Are there religious factors that should be considered?

Ways to better engage your audience.

There are several things you can do to prepare at the beginning of your speech that will help you engage better with the audience.

Research in Advance

Before you present, talk to the event's sponsors or organisers to find out how well-versed the audience is in the subject at hand. Inquire about their expectations and demographics, including their age, background, gender, and other details. If you're giving a presentation at an industry event, check out the event's website to learn about the event's mission and typical attendees. If you need to present in an organisation, learn as much as you can about them by visiting their website, reading news reports, and reviewing their blogs.

Be familiar with the room layout.

It is always an advantage to visit the location of your presentation. Find out, if possible, how the room will be laid out and if you could make any requests for positioning the visual aid equipment. The venue and the size of the room will give the speaker some idea as to how energetic and physical he will have to be to engage the audience, whether a microphone will be needed, and what type of visual aids will be the most effective.

Greet your audience at the door.

If you are unable to find out much information about the audience prior to the meeting, you may have to improvise and adjust your talk based on the information you collect at the beginning of the meeting. *Toastmasters International,* a non-profit educational organization that teaches public speaking suggests greeting people at the door and asking questions to ascertain their level of knowledge and expectations.

Using audience analysis, a speech is tailored to the interests, comprehension level, attitudes, and beliefs of its audience. It is important to take an audience-centred approach because a speaker's effectiveness will be improved if the presentation is created and delivered in an appropriate manner. You may come across a wide range of audiences:

Hostile and Disagreeable

Audiences of this type could be hostile and disagree with you.

- Work hard in building their trust and interest.
- Construct your presentation from an area of agreement or point of disagreement.
- Use humour.

Critical

Another type of audience you might expect is extremely critical, particularly at technical conferences. To deal with this kind of an audience:

- Use lots of evidence with strong references
- Argue both sides of the case, clearly stating the pros and cons of each.
- Try not to exaggerate; keep to the facts.

Uninformed

You will most likely come across audiences of this kind. They might have some idea about the subject of your presentation, but not much.

- Open up with questions so you can understand the level of knowledge that your audience has on the 'topic' you present.

- Spend a few slides going over the basics of your topic.

- Use simple language and avoid acronyms.

- Give basic facts and try to relate information to something people understand.

Sympathetic

This audience wants to be there and is willing to listen. They can be interested in your topic, excited to see you talk, and have an emotional attachment—these people are the easiest to persuade.

- Use the state of this audience to ask for help/funding etc.

- Trigger emotions which powerful stories

Audience Expectations

It's possible for different audiences to have very different expectations regarding the speaker and the topics. Your speech may suffer if you ignore these differences.

Knowledge of the Subject

You must determine how much your audience already knows about your subject because audiences' levels of knowledge can vary greatly. Never overestimate the audience's level of understanding. On the other hand, a speech that comes across as condescending could be one that grossly underestimates the level of knowledge held by the audience.

Audience Size

When speaking to a group of five people, it's often appropriate to use everyday language. When speaking to 500 people, though, you'll need a well-thought-out structure and the right methods. It is common practice to speak to large audiences from an elevated platform and with a microphone.

Demographics

The demographic factors of an audience include the following:

- Age
- Gender
- Religion
- Ethnic background
- Class
- Job or Career
- Education

These categories often determine the individual's experience and beliefs, so you should tailor your speech accordingly. Presenting at a conference in Boston will be a very different experience from presenting in Singapore. The structure of your speech and the words you use will probably be very different. However, the speech's objective need not be altered for each audience when demographic factors are used as a guide; Instead, you need to think about the information that will be most important to people from various demographic groups.

How to Connect with the Audience Individuals During a Presentation

It is quite a challenge to hold the audience's attention for the entire presentation. According to a study, half of the audience is likely to do something else other than listening to a presentation, things such as:

- Sending text/WhatsApp messages (28%)
- Checking emails (27%)
- Falling asleep (17%)

An interactive presentation has a much better chance of keeping the audience's attention and developing a rapport with them. There are a few easy ways to accomplish this, such as live polling and asking questions.

Listening to a presentation for any length of time could be tedious for the audience. If you do not involve the audience, they will get distracted, be occupied with their phones, talk to people sitting next to them, and generally lose track of the topic being presented. Once this happens, as a presenter, you start feeling anxious and might try to speed up the presentation.

To keep a fairly large audience engaged, your presentation needs to be lively, spontaneous, purposeful, and staged, as if it is a kind of conversation between both you and your audience. That way, the audience will not only absorb your ideas but 'take away' significant parts of your presentation in the most enjoyable way.

Use An Easy-To-Follow Structure

While structuring your presentation, focus on keeping it simple, something which people find easy to follow. Start by introducing the core ideas and goals, give an overview or background, then elaborate on the various parts, draw logical conclusions or possible solutions, and wrap up by leaving your audience with a clear takeaway message.

Get the Audience Immediately Involved

Your audience will come to listen to your presentation in a variety of moods. You can begin by using a simple icebreaker to involve the listeners and get them focused on your presentation. For example, you may ask people to introduce themselves to their neighbours or make them identify two or three questions they would like to hear in the course of your presentation. You can even ask the audience questions during your presentation. Take occasional breaks during your presentation to interact with the audience. Ask rhetorical questions that will involve your audience by making them actively participate in your presentation. A presenter is, after all, a performer who constantly tries to win over the audience and convince them.

Let the Audience Soak in the Presentation. Do not rush or speak so fast that the audience is not able to make much of what you are trying to say. Rushing through a presentation is an easy mistake that many presenters make. People tend to speak faster when they are nervous, and although this is natural, it kills a presentation. Racing through the slides will only disorient them, so remember to breathe and relax. This will help the audience to follow the talk and will calm your nerves.

Convey Passion. How the audience reacts to a particular piece of information depends on how you present it and matching those expressions with the tone of your voice will arouse their enthusiasm.

Point the Laser Correctly. If you point the laser haphazardly all across the slide, all eyes will follow the laser. Use the laser judiciously to highlight each thing in turn and hold your arms consistently so that the audience can focus on that one thing you are pointing at.

The next chapter is about suspense created in a presentation to arouse the curiosity of the audience.

9

CREATING SUSPENSE IN A PRESENTATION

Curiosity & Surprise in Presentations

Curiosity arises from the desire to know. Curiosity is an emotion. Curiosity is a feeling that arises from the desire to acquire knowledge or information.

Curiosity as a behaviour and emotion has been the driving force behind the development of knowledge in the fields of science, language, and industry. As a presenter, you can arouse the curiosity of the audience with your presentation so that they remain attentive to your talk.

Tension and suspense are powerful emotional experiences in various contexts (such as music, film, literature, and everyday life). When we watch an engrossing movie or read an interesting book for the first time, are we not curious to know the end? Is there any point when you do not pay attention? Your awareness increases as the level of suspense goes up.

Similarly, for any presentation, it is important to keep

alive the curiosity of the audience. The presenter must not, therefore, give everything away in the title slide or at the beginning of a presentation. We need to add suspense to our presentation. A speaker must add surprise to a presentation. Surprise is emotion, and emotion is attention.

How would you grab the attention of the audience with Curiosity, Suspense, and Surprise in your Slide Presentations?

That is possible if, by postponing the outcome of the story, the presenter could evoke Suspense. The suspense could be built up in a manner such as, *"Don't tell them. Don't tell them. Still—don't tell them. Then tell them."* Curiosity may also be evoked by presenting the outcome before the preceding events. Movies and TV shows love to do that! Finally, the presenter can talk about an unexpected event to trigger a surprise.

The following **slide patterns** are based on these three drivers: curiosity, emotion, and attention.

The Title Slide

Does a title slide kindle the curiosity of the audience, keep them guessing, or surprise them? And would it not be too far-fetched to argue that the first impression is a crucial moment for you as a presenter? Use your first slide in a way that gives a cue to your conclusion. For example, your first slide could have the year 2023 written in bold and a sentence that could be: "This year will change our entire business model." Then, without elaborating on the year, you could continue with the evolution of your business model. Later in your presentation, the number comes back, and you elaborate on it. Another example could be the use of a date. You can place a highly visible slide with a date such as 23/7/2023. This, for sure, will trigger curiosity.

The Infographic Slide

Infographic slides are made for the screen. Infographics combine data and visual representation with analysis. They are a great way to enhance any presentation. They generally add power to a point the presenter makes. And they generate a second significant benefit. Using an infographic template from PowerPoint or Google Slides, you can easily create a straightforward infographic for your presentation.

Here is an example of an infographic slide template for PowerPoint presentations:

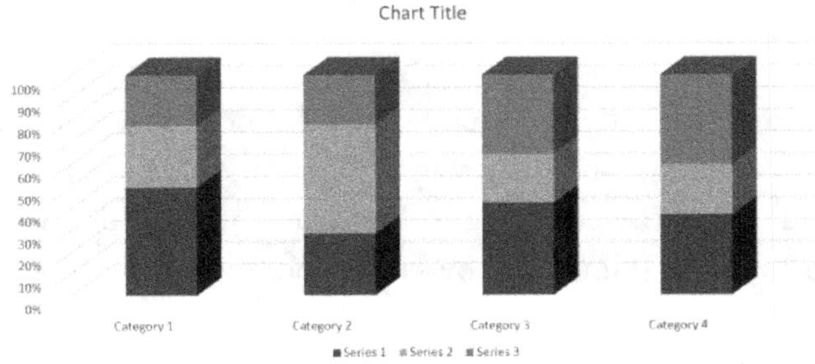

Air pollution infographics

Symptoms	Women	Men
Tiredness	50%	60%
Headache	100%	80%
Coughing	80%	60%
Difficulty breathing	30%	40%
Mucous	10%	15%
Irritation	70%	50%

BUSINESS PLAN INFOGRAPHICS

To catch the attention of your audience, you can mix curiosity with suspense in your infographic slides. First, you could begin by showing a structure with little or no information. Then, click by click, you add more details—from A to Z.

An expert in design and marketing once stated that the digital age had prepared us to provide visual proof through the steady presence of images that are readily available from multiple sources. Designers are quite aware that their job is to convey a message and get people to think or act in a certain way, not just make something look good.

Infographics used in presentations are intended to combine visual and verbal elements to strengthen communication. It takes 8 seconds for an average person to get distracted. By telling a visual story and by using numbers to validate our points, we have a much better chance of capturing our audience's attention.

The Punch Slide

Saying the unexpected is a standard pattern with which speakers can build expectations in the audience. They suddenly deviate and say something unexpected, which happens to be the punch line. You can also surprise your audience with unexpected images.

The Quiz Slide

Audiences love quizzes. The three attention-boosters, curiosity, suspense, and surprise, are all activated by Quiz Slides. Add quiz slides to your presentations. Surprise comes when you break the monotony. Black slides surprise the audience. A black slide will let the audience refocus on you, the presenter—instantly. In fact, the black slide makes a huge impact. The presence of simple infographics, equations with initials, punch slides, quizzes, and darkness, on the slides could trigger the curiosity of the audience, build suspense, and surprise them. Your audience's attention levels will rise significantly with your emotional impact.

10

PRACTICE & TIME YOUR PRESENTATION

We have seen how great actors perform on stage. They rehearse their scripted lines for days and then speak naturally and perform their part, keeping the audience enthralled and asking for more. A presenter's job is similar. A presenter needs to speak naturally, be a conversational speaker, and present without rambling. And to be a natural speaker, a presenter needs to rehearse for days.

First, write down a well-defined script and then write down the main ideas in the notes section of your PowerPoint slides. Underline the keywords and practice. Remember one keyword per slide. After adequate practice for several days, practice only from the slides and now without the notes. If you have enough practice, you will not require the notes to present. You will be confident to present.

Practice For Success

Since presentation is a kind of 'performance', it is also

important to overcome stage fright and gain confidence. Days of gruelling practice will bring you success. Practice in an empty room where you imagine people sitting so that you can move your eyes around the room to this "audience". To start with, focus on putting your outlined notes into full sentences in your natural voice. Never read your notes aloud. Now and then, you may take a brief glance down at your notes and then look up.

Practice two or three times and time yourself. If your presentation is much too long, edit it and leave out the irrelevant parts. Rehearse but never memorise and maintain a natural conversational tone.

Pay Attention to The Time

During a presentation, it is important to stay within your allotted time if you want to show respect for your audience and those who invited you to speak. Additionally, you will lose the audience's attention if you go overtime or cut it too fine.

There is probably a specific timeframe within which you must complete your speech. Set a timer during rehearsals and determine beforehand how long your speech should take.

Practice With a Timer

Arrange your time to prepare the first draft, and then ask yourself these questions:

- *Am I elaborating on the minor points too much?*

- *Do I have sufficient justifications for the main points? Do I require better examples or additional data? Where would visual aids have the greatest impact?*

- *Are my words appropriate for this subject? Do I have enough interesting points to add to the discussion of the subject? Should I speak informally?*

- *Is there cohesion that flows smoothly from one point to the next? Do I need a better introduction or transition to switch between ideas?*

Whatever you do, make sure you know exactly how long you will have to present, and therefore prepare accordingly. Logistics may not be within your control, so try to reduce your speaking time considerably. There is nothing worse than showing up for a talk expecting to have 60 minutes, only to learn that the norm is to have a 45-minute talk followed by a 15-minute Q&A. It is always best to practice keeping in mind the time limit. Monitor your time during a presentation and wear a watch. Place your watch on a table if there is one or wear it on the inside of your wrist. You can also use a smartphone to keep a note of the time. Prepare two versions of your presentation, one long and one short. Be ready to switch if a situation calls. It is also a good idea to reconfirm your speaking time with your host.

Allow time for questions. Entertain questions at the end of your presentation. Sometimes if the audience wants to hear more about the subject, continue during break time. Good time management is a sign of respect towards your audience.

Keep Practicing

The key to a good performance in practice. Practice changes in your style of delivery to emphasise key points. Don't keep looking at your notes. It is perfectly fine if you use words that are different from those you wrote down—the more you rehearse without looking at your notes, the more natural you will sound. Practice your pitch, your body language, how you walk around, how you use your hands, and where you point the laser. Although practising can be time-consuming, it will boost your self-confidence. The rule of thumb is to be so familiar with your talk that you will not miss a beat even if the computer fails or if there is a power disruption and none of your slides are visible. *Remember, practice is the most important part of delivering an interactive presentation. You need to rehearse over and over again and understand where to use live quizzes and when to accept questions, which points to emphasise and simultaneously be attentive about the use of your body language.*

11

THE IMPORTANCE OF BODY LANGUAGE

We have discussed the importance of a narrative in a presentation supported by words and slides. We have also discussed how the practice could make your presentation perfect. As you rehearse your presentation, pay special attention to your detailed body language and delivery style, which would possibly leave a lasting impression on your audience. *What* you say is important, but *how* you say it is equally important, if not more. Build your stage presence and rehearse till you are able to present effortlessly.

Non-verbal communication plays a large part in how we construct meaning, so it is important to consider how best to use the same in your presentation. You can make things more interesting for your audience by using the right body language to enhance your talk. Body language goes beyond reinforcing your messaging. 'Assertive' body language increases confidence and decreases stress. An effective presenter pays close attention to a kind of physical connectivity with his audience. If you stand too far away from your audience, they will not develop a bond with you, and this will limit the effectiveness of your presentation. At the same time, you also need to emotionally connect with them through your words and body language.

Enthusiasm, Postures, Gestures, & Emphasis

Your posture could dictate levels of audience involvement. If you are too slackened and sit drooped on a chair to present your speech, the crowd could possibly float away. Find a comfortable but purposeful position in relation to your audience and adopt an upright sitting or standing posture that allows for movement and gesture. Always keep your posture open, stay animated on your feet, and do not take shelter in one corner behind your laptop or computer. Bring unlimited energy to your presentation. Audiences respond well to the physical energy and enthusiasm being conveyed by a presenter. Gestures that are open and reach out to your audience extend your presentation to them and thus help them feel more involved. Use gestures when emphasising key points. Use calm, deliberate movements when highlighting certain information, and keep your arms and legs uncrossed. An enthusiastic presenter, through his body language, can create enthusiasm in the listeners and motivate them to pay attention, ask questions, collaborate, and communicate.

Eye Contact

Eye contact may be the most significant physical action onstage. Move your eyes to the people who give positive vibes as you begin the presentation. Making eye contact with the audience is one of the most powerful techniques for involving them. Great communicators and presenters make eye contact with the audience all the time. As you talk to your audience, maintain eye contact with them. Eye contact is associated with transparency, trustworthiness, and sincerity. If used well, eye contact can serve to make your address much more personal and effective. Average presenters try to break eye contact with the audience. If eye contact is avoided, the presenter can appear nervous and unconvincing. Eye contact will help you connect with the audience and make them feel they are a part of your presentation. The more you know your content inside out, the easier it will be for you to make eye contact with your listeners.

Maintaining an Audible Tone & Pace

One of the elements of a good presentation is maintaining an audible tone to make sure that it clearly reaches out to every member of the audience. A good way to improve audibility is to bring about voice modulation and to make sure that words are articulated and enunciated as clearly as possible. How people hear your message is influenced by the tone of your voice, volume, and other aspects. Bring some variation to your vocal delivery. You need to raise and lower your pitch as required. Your vocal delivery could add suspense and drama to your content. Be careful about your choice of words, words that you would like to use for emphasis. With poor delivery, your presentation will fall flat in the face. Pay attention to pause, pitch, and voice modulation.

Modulate Your Voice

Learn to use intonation. For example, when you ask a question, use a high note at the end. Finish on a low note whenever you make a declarative statement. These things usually happen naturally, but they can get lost when you are nervous.

Pause

A pause at the right time would not only arouse curiosity but will give time for the points to sink in. A good presentation relies heavily on maintaining a steady pace. This gives the listeners enough time to comprehend the material, take notes, and ask questions. A good presenter should learn not to speak too quickly because the audience requires time to understand what is being communicated. At the same time, the pace should not be so slow that, as a presenter, you run out of time to complete the presentation!

Develop Stage Presence

For inexperienced speakers, the physical act of being onstage can be the most difficult part of giving a presentation—but people tend to overestimate its importance. Getting the words, story, and substance right is a much bigger determinant of success or failure than how you stand or whether you are visibly nervous. And when it comes to stage presence, practice can take you a long way. People sway from side to side or shift their weight from one leg to the other, which is a common mistake we see in the early rehearsals. During a presentation, there are some people who walk around the stage, which can be very distracting. However, for the vast majority, it is preferable to remain still and emphasise through hand gestures.

A presenter must practice standing tall with open hands and relaxed movements. Being a presenter, be careful about making use of eye contact, the most important body language in a presentation. Be careful enough not to clutter up all your PowerPoint slides with too many details. The result is we end locked up in our slides, repeating the slide content. We sound stiff and wooden and forget to connect with the audience. The best way therefore is to elaborate the points in simple, clear, understandable language using a conversational style with the audience.

Body Language in a Presentation	
A presenter's desired Body Language-Do's	**Body Language to avoid during a presentation- Don'ts**
1. Dress professionally 2. Face the audience 3. Consider your postures and gestures. 4. Use open hand	1. Do not fidget. 2. Do not put your hands in your pocket. 3. Avoid wrong gestures by folding your hands and pacing up and down the podium. 4. Avoid looking at the screen

gestures.	continuously.
5. Make eye contact randomly with all sections of the audience.	5. Do not read from the screen.
6. Be confident and look confident.	6. Do not panic and show your anxiety

Overcoming Nervousness

Another big hurdle for inexperienced speakers is nervousness—prior to the talk and on stage. But the single best advice is simply to breathe deeply before going on stage. It really helps. In general, people worry too much about nervousness. Nerves are not a disaster. The audience *expects* you to be nervous. It is natural and can actually improve your performance: It gives you the energy to perform and keeps your mind sharp. Just keep breathing, and you will be fine.

Overcoming Anxiety

Even though some people seem to be good public speakers, most of us, at least at the very beginning, have some stage fright or anxiety about speaking to a group. You might feel that everybody is looking at you and judging you for every mistake you make, and this makes you all the more nervous, and you tend to forget what you actually want to say. But you can learn to overcome your anxiety and prepare in a way that will not only give you confidence but also lead you to make a successful presentation. Here are some strategies for overcoming anxiety when speaking in public:

- **Understand anxiety.** Anxiety can inspire you to prepare well and give your best. Learn to live with this part of the process and work to get around it. Tension mounts up when you are about to start but gradually eases out.

- **Reduce anxiety by preparing and practising.** The more you prepare, and the more you rehearse, the more you will be able to overcome your anxiety.

- **Focus on the content and delivery style.** Focus on the content of your presentation and be aware of how you deliver the same. Do not speak too fast, pause where necessary, and use a conversational style.

- **Develop self-confidence.** It is best to write down the points and refer to those during practice. You will become more self-assured as you practice.

If you are still nervous, take a few deep breaths. Rehearse your opening lines in your mind. Most importantly, keep your eyes moving over the audience. Practice smiling and pausing at key points. Smiling helps to relax both you and the audience. In addition to giving you a relaxed and calm appearance, smiling makes you feel good. Move to the front of the room and smile as you look at your audience. As a presenter, you need to learn how best to impact the audience with your presence and presentation. It is as important as the work that goes behind researching it. A presentation comprises of information and show. You need to put forth information before the audience, but you also need to create an impact in the mind of the audience with style and élan, the right attitude, and the most appropriate body movements.

$$12$$

MAKING A CLASSROOM PRESENTATION

Presentations made in the classroom can form a natural part of task-based learning. By focusing on a particular language point or skill, a presentation is a remarkably interesting way to learn, revise, and extend pair and group work.

Presentation As a Tool for Acquiring the Four Language Skills

Presentation could be an incredible method to make students practice different areas of language learning (vocabulary, grammar, discourse, and phonology) and language skills (speaking, reading, writing and listening).

Young learners develop their confidence with each new opportunity to present and sharpen their skills in presenting. In fact, a presentation can be used as a channel for students to share with others what they have learned during the course of their study. By allowing other people to ask questions, it also gives them a chance to test themselves and improve their understanding of the subject.

Guidelines for Presentations

Preparing and delivering a presentation in class can be a part of a successful learning process. Here are a few steps:

1. *Plan, and organise your content.*
2. *Prepare speaking notes.*
3. *Add relevant slides for visuals with minimal content.*
4. *Draft and revise the presentation.*
5. *Plan an introduction and conclusion.*
6. *Practice the presentation.*
7. *Deliver the presentation.*

Who Will See and Hear Your Class Presentation—And why?

In a class, who else will hear your presentation but the other students and the instructor? However, you still need to think about what they already know or what they do not know and what new things you ought to bring before them. If your topic of presentation is a subject matter taught in class lectures and readings, consider what background information they already have and be careful not to repeat the things they already know. It may be important, however, to show how your specific topic fits in with subjects that have already been discussed and taught in class.

You may be acquainted with new terms and concepts during your research and preparation but remember to explain and elaborate them to the audience, i.e., to your classroom peers.

Provide a simple explanation with relevant examples for the audience to grasp your points. If your topic involves anything controversial or may provoke emotion, take into consideration the audience's attitudes, and choose your words carefully. Be sure you are clear about the goals for the presentation. Are you primarily presenting new information or arguing to justify your point? Your presentation will be guided by your objectives in every way: what you say, how you say it, how much you say it, what visuals you use, whether you use humour or personal examples, and so forth.

Plan, and Organise your Content

Beginning with the objectives and the assignment, and your goals, analyse your topic. Jot down notes on specific topics that seem important. Often take notes as you would with any reading. Do not be concerned at first about how much information you're gathering as you research the subject at this stage. It is better to gather the maximum information and then edit, keeping only the most important things you would like to present.

Organizing a presentation is the first step. Introduce your topic and state your main idea, go into more detail about specific ideas, and conclude your presentation. Here too, you need to look for a logical order while presenting, as discussed in the previous chapter. While researching your topic and outlining your main points think about visual aids that may help the presentation. Also, start thinking about how much time you have for the presentation, but do not limit yourself to the outline stage.

The content being presented, the time of day, the grade level, and so on all affect how a presentation is structured. One thing that will not vary is the need to grab the attention of the audience (students) from the very beginning.

A three-stage process makes it easy to follow.

- **Stage 1**: Identify the key message of a topic you have selected and what you want your fellow classmates to remember. You can have a number of supporting arguments but just one key message. Time your speech.

- **Stage 2**: Identifying the arguments to support your message. Avoid excess details due to time constraints. Do emphasise clarity and precision.

- **Stage 3**: Identifying what is important to arouse the interest of the class.

Practice your speech as many times as necessary to build confidence. Practice your discourse many times to till you gain confidence. Practice but do not memorise. You may rehearse and record. Practice makes one less nervous.

Preparing Speaking Notes

Speaking notes could help provide a brief outline for your classroom presentation. You might write them on index cards or sheets of paper. Include important facts and data as well as keywords for your main ideas. It is not a good idea to read your presentation from a written page. Speak naturally—and you can never do this if you keep your eyes on a written script.

You need to plan how you will open and close your presentation because these two moments make the greatest impact on the whole presentation. Use the opening to capture the attention of your class.

You can relate the opening of your topic and your main point and move into the body of the presentation. You need to make a gradual transition from your last point to a brief summary that pulls your ideas together before you end the presentation. You might end up challenging the audience in class with a strong statement about your topic or a personal reflection on what you have been saying.

Strategies for Creating Interactive Presentations

Here are some strategies for creating a presentation with interactive components:

Sharing

In classroom presentations, students may be selected randomly or have them take turns in some kind of order. A classroom presentation is a learning activity for students, and not everyone will get it right the very first time.

Benefits of Having Interactive Components in Your Presentation

Retention: Actively having students engage with the concepts of the presentation in different ways and hearing it from different people (besides the teacher) helps in long-term retention.

Fun: Having a break from the routine, getting a chance to move around, developing teams, and sharing are much more enjoyed by students than passively listening to lectures and taking notes.

Feedback: Adding interactive activities into a presentation gives you instant feedback about students' comprehension.

Voicing opinion: Having students actually voice their ideas helps them to internalise the concepts in a better way.

Students who make classroom presentations should not keep looking at their watch. Practice will help you keep within your specified time. At the close of a presentation, deliver your last line with confidence, sweeping your eyes over your peers in the class. Before you wrap up, ask if there are any questions. When you are done, pause, smile, say "Thank you," and walk back to your seat.

But do not forget to ask other students and your teacher for comments. If you hear a suggestion for improvement, store it in your memory for the very next time you present.

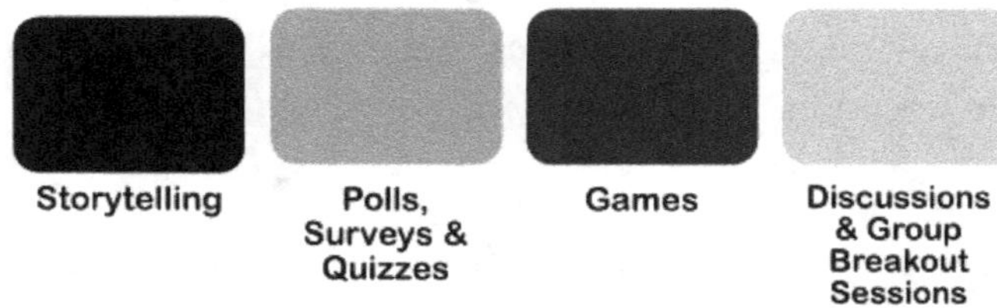

13

PREPARING FOR A GROUP PRESENTATION

Sometimes presentations happen in small groups. The six-step process discussed in the previous chapters works well for group presentations, too, although group dynamics often call for additional planning and shared responsibilities:

To get started, set up a group meeting as soon as possible.

In **step one** of a group presentation, begin by:

a) *Analyse your audience and your goals together as a group to make sure everyone understands the assignment with clarity.*

b) *Discuss who should do what.*

c) *While everyone should talk about what content to include, from here onwards, you will take on specialised roles.*

d) *One or two of the members may begin research and gathering information.*

e) *Others who are good writers may volunteer to draft the presentation,*

f) *while one or more others may develop visual aids.*

g) *Those who have public speaking experience may volunteer to do all or most of the speaking (unless the assignment requires everyone to have a speaking role).*

h) *There might be a need for a team leader to keep everyone on schedule, organise meetings, and so on. An even-tempered student with good social skills who can inspire team members to work together is the best leader.*

Steps two and **three** could be carried out individually with assigned tasks, but group members should stay in touch with each other. For instance, in order to determine the required visuals and begin the search for or creation of them, the person developing the visuals must coordinate with those conducting research and drafting.

Before preparing notes in **step four**, group members must meet again, go over the content and plan for visuals. Everyone should be comfortable with the plan.

The entire presentation should be divided into segments, and each presenter should be allocated a segment to speak on. The time for each segment should be clearly set. The speakers should prepare their own speaking notes. Someone with strong speaking skills could open or close the presentation (or both), with others doing the other parts.

The whole group should be present for practice sessions

in **step five**, even if everyone is not speaking. Those who are not speaking ought to provide feedback and take notes. If one student is doing most of the presentation, an alternate student should be kept ready in case the first student is unable to present on the scheduled day owing to some unforeseen circumstances.

During the delivery, especially if using technology for visual aids, one student should manage the visuals while others would do the presenting. If several students present different segments, the transition should be gradual from one to another so that the presentation keeps flowing without breaks.

When using technology for showing visual aids in a presentation, one student is expected to manage the visuals while others deliver the talk. However, the presentation must continue uninterrupted and the transition gradual, even when multiple students present different segments in a group presentation.

Answer Questions Thoughtfully

All presenters need to remain relaxed during the question period. Remember, as experts on the subject presented, this is a chance to demonstrate your expertise on the subject presented. The audience is not expected to harass you during the question period. Your audience is supportive and interested, and they genuinely want to know more about the topic. Anyone from the group can take the questions and answer them. When answering questions, be composed and make sure you understand the question clearly before you answer. If the question is not understood, you must gently ask for clarification.

Prior to your talk, think carefully about the presentation so that you are able to anticipate major questions. If you can predict that something, in particular, will come up, prepare an answer beforehand. If you are unable to answer a question, try to say something useful and relevant. "*I don't know*" is perfectly acceptable if you truly do not know, but not for every question.

14

CREATING A POSTER PRESENTATION

Most scientific conferences and workshops offer a scope of poster presentations. This medium of exposition of one's research work has its own advantages.

In an oral presentation, one gets a fixed amount of time to discuss one's work, and this window of interaction is the same for all members of the audience. One cannot personalise the interaction depending on the interest of individual listeners. However, in a poster session, one may limit interaction to a brief summary for people who are only interested in learning "what it is all about", while those who are really interested to know the specific details of the work may engage in extensive discussion.

Preparing the Poster

In order to create an effective poster presentation, the poster must be well-designed. The material to be put on the poster should be carefully considered. Remember, nobody is going to read the whole poster. You will explain, standing in front of the poster. So put in only those issues, mostly as bullet points, that you would need to refer to while explaining. The overall look of the poster should have an aesthetic appeal.

If a poster catches the eye from a distance, it is more likely to be spotted by those who might be interested in your work. One can easily look up good examples of scientific poster design through Google search. One can make a poster as one PowerPoint slide if one is working in a Windows environment. LATEX offers many packages specifically designed for this purpose. Every conference and workshop specifies the allowed size of the poster. Start by setting these dimensions right. Then copy and paste your own material into the template. Make sure all texts in the poster are readable from at least 1.5 metres. The suggested font sizes are title: 60 points, section headings: 30 points, text: no smaller than 20 points. Select a sans-serif font (e.g., Helvetica, Arial) for titles and headings. If there are equations, choose a font for the running text that does not look too different from the font used in the equations (i.e., they should be from the same font family). The poster should be dominated by graphs, charts, and similar pictures, not by text.

Presenting A Poster

Keep in mind that the majority of conference attendees will only have a passing interest in your poster work, and only a select few would be truly interested. The whole art of presenting a poster is to attract interested people to your poster and have a fruitful interaction with them.

The usual mistake that many presenters make is to grab somebody who drifted to the poster and lecture him/her for half an hour. This person may not be really interested in the work but cannot move away because of courtesy. Worse, another person who might be really interested may see that you are in the middle of an elaborate explanation and may not like to join in at that stage. So, prepare a brief outline that can be presented in 3-4 minutes, meant for most people who come to your poster. It should tell the listener what it is all about, what scientific questions you are addressing, what is your methodology of investigation, and what are the prime conclusions of the work.

Go into further details only if the listener shows interest and asks questions. There will be a few people who may be working in areas directly related to yours or may be interested in your work due to other reasons. You should aim to have a more elaborate discussion with them, explaining the details. It is a good idea to keep a laptop computer with you so that if a question comes up that will require you to refer to something not in the poster (for example, the detailed arrangement of an experiment or a video), you might be able to show it.

15

THINGS TO REMEMBER

The Takeaway Message

As you are about to wrap up your presentation, share a motivational story as the takeaway message for your presentation. By the end of your presentation, the audience will have remembered the compelling stories, case studies, and customer experiences you have shared with them, depending on how interestingly you have presented them. Your information will be etched in their minds for an exceptionally long time to come.

A Surprise at the End

As you wind up, the attention of the audience considerably fades away. You can re-activate their attention by surprising them with data or information they have not anticipated.

A Rhetorical Question

A provocative or controversial question at the end will stimulate the audience's mind as they will require some amount of brainstorming to find the answer.

Wind up with an Impactful Visual

In the end, you can use a persuasive visual relevant to your presentation that will convey the take-home message, one that will help them remember the very essence of your presentation.

Wrap Up with A Summary and Closing Remark.

You need to summarise the key points of your presentation once again at the end. Summarise in style by adding catchy ending phrases, humour, or anecdote. An animated slide with motion effects will help create a visual impact and intensify the key takeaways. Avoid making an abrupt wrap-up. Finish your presentation with a call to action and illustrate it visually on the slide. Use a closing remark. Your closing will clearly state that the presentation is over. Devote a little time to make your ending perfect and leave your audiences fascinated, enthralled, and wanting more.

REFERENCES

1. Butterfield S. A talk on giving talks: Tips to ace medical lectures. 2015 Retrieved from http://www.acpinternist.org/archives/2015/06/talk.htm

2. LearnFree.org. Simple rules for better PowerPoint presentations. 2017 Retrieved from http://www.gcflearnfree.org/powerpoint-tips/simple-rules-for-better-powerpoint-presentations/

3. Marinho A C F, de Medeiros A M, Gama A C C, Teixeira L C. Fear of public speaking: Perception of college students and correlates. Journal of Voice. 2016;31(1): 127.e7–127.e11. [PubMed] [Google Scholar]

4. Gallo, Carmine. The Presentation Secrets of Steve Jobs. McGraw Hill LLC. 2009

5. Atkinson, Cliff. Beyond Bullet Points. Pearson Education. 2011

INKFEATHERS PUBLISHING

www.inkfeathers.com

We love creating beautiful books for you!

Come be a part of our ever-growing community of authors. Grow, write, and publish with us!

Scan here to explore books, authors and more

Connect with us on socials. We'd love to hear from you!

    Inkfeathers Publishing

www.ingramcontent.com/pod-product-compliance
Lightning Source LLC
La Vergne TN
LVHW011058200726
843510LV00003B/915